Contenido

Contents

¡Las palas mecánicas son fantásticas! Mueven la tierra y otras cosas.

Bulldozers are cool! They move dirt and other things.

EN
construcción
Construction
SITE

LAS PALAS MECÁNICAS
BULLDOZERS

SPANISH

Dan Osier

Traducción al español: Eida de la Vega

PowerKiDS press.

New York

Published in 2014 by The Rosen Publishing Group, Inc.
29 East 21st Street, New York, NY 10010

First Edition

Editor: Amelie von Zumbusch
Book Design: Andrew Povolny   Traducción al español: Eida de la Vega

Photo Credits: Cover Jelle vd Wolf/Shutterstock.com; p. 5 Jan van Broekhoven/Shutterstock.com; p. 7 Guido Akster/Shutterstock.com; p. 9 Asaf Eliason/Shutterstock.com; pp. 11, 15, 17, 23 iStockphoto/Thinkstock; p. 13 Tomasz Pietryszek/Photodisc/Getty Images; p. 19 JoLin/Shutterstock.com; p. 21 Jupiterimages/Photos.com/Thinkstock.

Library of Congress Cataloging-in-Publication Data

Osier, Dan.
Bulldozers = Las palas mecánicas / by Dan Osier ; translated by Eida de la Vega. — First edition.
    pages cm. — (Construction site = En construcción)
English and Spanish.
Includes index.
ISBN 978-1-4777-3283-0 (library)
1. Bulldozers—Juvenile literature. I. Vega, Eida de la. II. Osier, Dan. Bulldozers. III. Osier, Dan. Bulldozers. Spanish. IV. Title. V. Title: Palas mecánicas.
TA725.O8518 2014
629.225—dc23
                          2013022463

Websites: Due to the changing nature of Internet links, PowerKids Press has developed an online list of websites related to the subject of this book. This site is updated regularly. Please use this link to access the list:
www.powerkidslinks.com/cs/dozers/

Manufactured in the United States of America

CPSIA Compliance Information: W14PK3: For Further Information contact Rosen Publishing, New York, New York at 1-800-237-9932

Algunas se usan en la construcción. Otras se usan en minas y granjas.

Some are used in construction. Others are used in mines or on farms.

Algunos ejércitos las usan. La que usa el ejército de Israel se llama Doobi.

Some armies use them. The nickname for an Israeli Army one is a Doobi.

Las pala mecánicas son lentas.
Las más rápidas van a 18
millas por hora (29 km/h).

They are slow. The fastest
ones go just 18 miles per
hour (29 km/h).

Muchas palas mecánicas tienen **orugas**. Ellas impiden que las palas mecánicas se hundan en el suelo blando.

Bulldozers tend to have **tracks**. These keep bulldozers from sinking into soft soil.

La **hoja de empuje** está en el frente. Se usa para empujar cosas.

The **blade** is in front. It pushes things.

Hay tres tipos de hojas.
La hoja S, la hoja U y la hoja S-U.

There are three kinds of blades.
They are the S blade, the U
blade, and the S-U blade.

Algunas palas mecánicas tienen **escarificadores**. Están detrás. Rompen la tierra.

Some bulldozers have **rippers**. They are on the back. They tear up dirt.

Muchas compañías hacen palas mecánicas. La mayoría las hace Caterpillar.

Many companies make bulldozers. Caterpillar makes the most.

¿Has visto alguna vez una pala mecánica?

Have you ever seen a bulldozer?

PALABRAS QUE DEBES SABER / WORDS TO KNOW

(la) hoja de empuje

blade

(el) escarificador

ripper

(la) oruga

track

ÍNDICE

INDEX